Introduction.

This book follows on from Book 1 - 'Flowers and (expanding the applications of some of the origin: latest range of small flower cutters,showing how t(use and versatility.

Full details of our cutters R1 to R14 are contained in Book 1. Some of the terms used in this book are also fully described in Book 1.

There are many ways of making sugar flowers, but the methods shown in this book have been tried and tested with many students and are designed to ensure a successful result first time. However, practice makes perfect and everyone can improve!

The Tools

General Notes.

Non-Stick.	One of the most useful aspects of their design is their non-stick property which is inherent in the material used. It is not a surface finish and, therefore, cannot wear off.
Materials.	All the tools can be used with any soft material such as flowerpaste, sugarpaste, marzipan,modelling chocolate, plasticine, modelling clay etc.
Temperature.	They will withstand boiling water or the dishwasher without deforming.
Handles.	All the cutters have comfortably sized hollow handles which allow you to exert firm pressure over the whole of the cutting edges.
Stability.	They will not rust, corrode, deform or wear out with normal useage.
Marking.	All the tools are permanently marked to aid easy identification,and are packed in clear hang-up bags.
Metal.	They should not be brought into contact with sharp metal objects which may damage the cutting edges or surfaces i.e keep them separated from metal cutters.
Boards.	Our non-stick boards and non-stick rolling pins,with their rubber feet, really do make handling sticky materials more of a pleasure and enable you to roll out your pastes much thinner than you thought possible.
Hygiene.	The materials meet the appropriate EEC Regulations for food hygiene.
Endorsement.	All the items are personally endorsed and used by Pat Ashby,our Technical Director, who is one of the leading teachers in this country and is an International Judge.

NEW GREEN NON-STICK BOARDS.

You will see in some of the illustrations our new GREEN non-stick board,which is slightly more restful on your eyes and,for Tutors,shows up white pastes much better. They are available in the same standard range of sizes as the white boards: Ref.30-5″x6¾″, Ref.31-10″x6¾″, Ref.32-12″x9½″, and Ref.33-24″x19″.

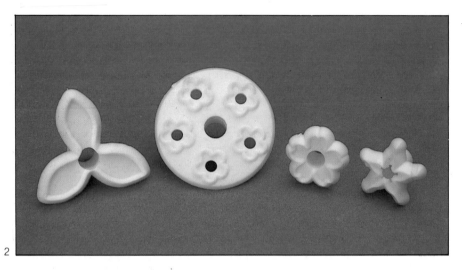

THE NEW CUTTERS
(Full size cutout shapes shown in Illustration 3)

Ref.6: Small Calyx Cutter (R15) 19mm
(N.B. The Mk 2 version has a large hole through the handle allowing the 'Mexican Hat' method of cutting to be used. This version is marked R̄15.

This cutter extends our existing range of Calyx cutters(R11-R13) to a smaller size in the same style with an equally attractive shape.

The metric dimension shown is intended to give you some idea as to the actual size of the cutter, the word 'small' being fairly imprecise. It is the diameter of smallest circle into which the finished cutout will fit. The equivalent figures for our larger Calyxes are as follows;-

     Large Calyx (R11) 43mm
     Medium Calyx (R12) 36mm
     Minor Calyx (R13) 29mm

Ref.7: Freesia Cutter (F1)
This cutter,whose shape was taken from an actual flower, can be used with the 'Mexican Hat' method of cutting and makes delightful flowers easily.(See Page 13).

Ref.8: Blossom Cutter (F2)
This unique cutter cuts out 5- Blossoms simultaneously and can also be used to make attractive patterns quickly round the side of a cake or on a plaque. It does not stick,has no moving parts,cannot rust or corrode but does need to be used with very thin paste. This is as it should be since blossoms ought to be very delicate. The 5 was chosen so that you can cup all five before they begin to harden.(see Page 15).

Ref. 9: Small Primrose Cutter (F3)
This versatile and beautifully shaped cutter (again taken from an actual flower) can be used to make several different flowers, some of which may not have occured to you before. (See Pages 16-22).

R15

F1

F2

F3

3

4

How to make the Christmas Rose *(See Illustration 4)*

1. Roll out white flowerpaste very thinly-until you can see through it- and cut out 5 petals using the R2 cutter. Soften the edges with the balling tool (OP 1) and press out a little at the top to get a pointed shape. When dry dust the bottom of the petals with pale green petal dust using a soft brush.

2. To assemble,cut a 2½″ square of wax paper and make diagonal cuts towards the centre from each corner approx.1/3rd of the way in. Pipe a bulb of pale green Royal Icing in the centre. You can put the wax paper into an apple box if you wish.
   Place two of the petals(No's 1 & 2) opposite each other with their bottom edges meeting in the icing. Place petal No.3 overlapping No.1, and petal No.4 overlapping No's.3 & 2. Petal No.5 overlaps No's.1 & 2. i.e the flower is not symetrical (See Illustration 5).

3. Pipe a bulb of pale green Royal Icing in the centre and insert about 30 yellow-headed stamens.

4. When dry peel off the wax paper and position on the cake with a bulb of Royal Icing. In an arrangement a red wax candle will set off the pale flowers.

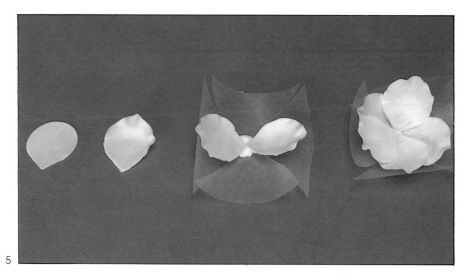

5

How to make a Christmas Table Decoration *(See Illustration 6)*

1. Roll out some pale green Sugarpaste or Pastillage and cut out a plaque with the base of the Petal Box. Allow to set.
2. Make a sausage of pale green Sugarpaste as a candle holder and glue in the centre of the plaque (use egg white,gum arabic or rose water). Push a small red wax candle into the centre to make a socket,remove and allow to dry.
3. Make some ribbon bows and tails. Insert the candle in the holder and arrange about 3 Christmas Roses around the candle interspersed with bows to complete the table decoration.

6

7

How to make the Wired Briar Rose *(See Illustration 7)*

1. Roll out a little green and white flowerpaste thinly, place one piece on top of the other and roll again. Cut out a large Calyx (R11) and soften the edges of the sepals with the balling tool (OP 1). Cup the sepals slightly with the balling tool.(See Illustration 8). Make a small hole in the centre of a plastic apple tray and the calyx,and lay on top of a glass or similar support. Place the calyx into the apple tray.
2. Roll out white paste very thinly and cut out 5 petals with the Briar Rose petal cutter (R14). Thin the edges with the balling tool but do not frill. Place them on a sponge dusted with cornflour and cup with a blunt tool.
3. Paint a touch of glue(egg white,gum arabic or rose water) in the centre of the calyx and along the adjacent sepals. Place the point of a petal onto the centre of the calyx (See Illustration 9). Continue glueing the remaining petals in the calyx overlapping each one, with the last tucking under the first.
4. Make a small hook in the end of a piece of 28 gauge wire and bend the top over. While the petals are still soft,apply a little glue to the centre of the flower, and push the wire through the centre and through the hole in the apple tray into the glass (See Illustration 10).

8

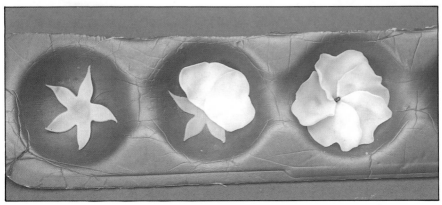

9

5. To make the centre take a small ball of yellow paste and mark it by pressing firmly against a piece of tulle. Insert a large number of stamens in multiples of five, of varying lengths with the longer curved ones on the outside and leaving a bare patch in the centre.
6. Apply a little glue to the centre of the flower and attach the centre piece. When dry, highlight each stamen with yellow petal dust and a touch of brown paste colour.
7. To wire the leaves (See Illustration 11), roll out some green flowerpaste slightly larger than the required leaf size and thicker than normal. Using a plastic knitting needle or similar thin out the sides and top to the required thickness leaving a thicker portion at the bottom. Cut out the leaf using Leaf Cutters R5, R6 or R7 keeping the thickened portion of the paste at the bottom. Then 'glue' the end of a piece of 28 gauge wire and, holding the leaf between your finger and thumb, push the end of the wire into the thickened portion, Vein the leaf by pressing onto the appropriate dusted Leaf Mould (R8, R9 or R10) and leave to dry.

10

11

12

How to make the Lily *(See Illustration 12)*

1. Make a small hook on the end of a piece of 28 gauge wire. Glue the hook with egg white,gum arabic or rose water and attach a sausage of yellow flowerpaste. The length of the sausage should be about 1/3 of the length of the petal cutter used (R1,R2,R3 or R4). Dip the paste into yellow mealie meal,semolina,gelatine or coloured caster sugar to represent pollen (See Illustration 45). Leave to dry.
2. Roll out white flowerpaste and cut out one petal using an R1,R2,R3 or R4 cutter as required. Soften the edges with the balling tool (OP 1). Apply glue halfway up from the base of the sausage and wrap the petal round, point at the top. Bend the top gently back. (See Illustration 13).
3. When dry dust the throat and back of the petal ¾ of the way up using yellow petal dust. Petal dust the outside of the base of the petal green.

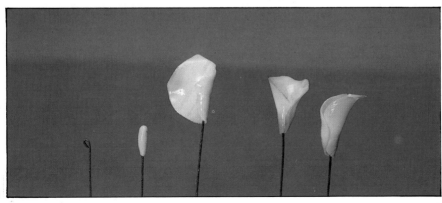

13

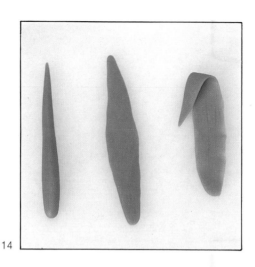

14

4. To make the leaves (See illustration 14). Roll out a thin tapered sausage of green flowerpaste and flatten it with the heel of your dusted hand. Vein it ,either by pressing onto a dried maize leaf(see Page 31) or by marking a few lines along its length with the back of a knife. Fold over the end and leave to dry.

How to make the Anemone *(See Illustration 15)*

1. Roll out some white flowerpaste and cut out 9 petals using the R2 Rose petal cutter. Soften the edges with the balling tool (OP 1). Lay them on a thick soft sponge dusted with cornflour and cup them with a blunt tool. When dry colour the top 1/3rd with petal dust(colour of choice) - keep the centre 1/3rd white - colour the bottom 1/3rd black at the point (See Illustration 16).
2. Cut a 2½″ square of wax paper diagonally in from the corners (approx. 1/3rd of the way in) and lay it in an apple tray. Pipe a circle of Royal Icing in the centre - about ½″ dia.- and lay 6 petals,points inwards, overlapping round it. (See Illustration 17).
3. Pipe another circle on top of the 6 petals and lay the remaining 3 in between the previous petals as a second layer.
4. Pipe a bulb of black Royal Icing in the centre and flatten it slightly. Curve some black stamens of varying lengths and insert them round the icing with tweezers. Leave the centre clear.

15

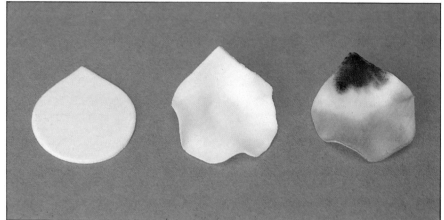

16

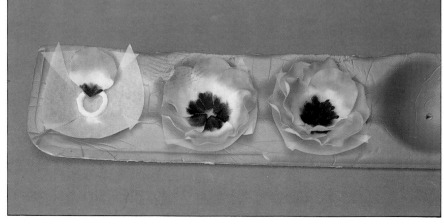

17

9

18

How to make the Pansy *(See Illustration 18)*

1. Roll out coloured flowerpaste thinly and cut out 5 petals using the R4 cutter.(If you wish to make them larger use R3,R2 or R1). Soften the edges and cup the centres of the first two petals with the balling tool(OP 1).
2. Place petal No.1 into an apple tray and apply a little 'glue'(egg white,gum arabic or rose water) to the righthand side at the base. Lay the lefthand side of petal No.2 overlapping No.1.(See Illustration 19).
3. Soften the edges of petal No.3,cup your dusted hand and ball the centre of the petal with a circular motion.Slightly flute the edges with a cocktail stick. Turn the petal over and cup. Apply glue to the lefthand side of petal No.1 and place petal No.3 overlapping No.1.
4. Treat petal No.4 in the same way, glue righthand side of petal No.2 and overlap No.4 on No.2.
5. Treat petal No.5 in the same way as No.3,glue the unoccupied sides of petals No's 3 & 4 and place No.5 overlapping both. Indent the centre of the flower with a cocktail stick and pipe a 'V' at the base of the indentationin yellow Royal Icing using a '0' tube,starting halfway up with the point of the V at the base of the indentation.
6. Place black colour onto greaseproof paper and work the colour with a 'OO' paintbrush until smooth. Then paint the 'face' onto the pansy. When dry dust the edges with petal dust.

19

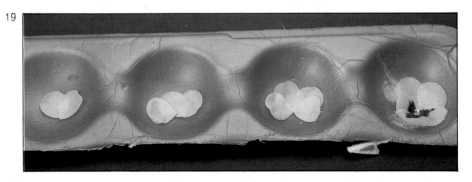

20

How to make the Christmas Tree *(See Illustration 20)*

1. Make a brown tub about ¾" diameter and ½" high from flowerpaste or Almond paste. Mark the sides with a knife. Push a 2½" length of 26 gauge wire(or the finest variety of spaghetti*) into the top to make a hole. Remove the wire and push into a firm base,such as a piece of polystyrene, to hold it steady while assembling. Slide a small ball of green flowerpaste over the wire down to where the top of the tub would come.
2. Roll out green flowerpaste and cut out 3 - Large Calyx(R11). Soften edges with the balling tool (OP 1) and cup each sepal working from the tip to the centre. Make a small hole in the centre of each calyx and leave to firm a little.
3. Put a little 'glue'(egg white,gum arabic or rose water) onto the green ball on the wire and slide the first calyx down the wire points uppermost.(See Illustration 21). Slide another small ball of green paste down the wire and repeat the process for the next two large calyxes making sure the points of each calyx are positioned between those of the one underneath.
4. Repeat this process with 3-Medium Calyx(R12),3-Minor Calyx(R13) and 3-Small Calyx(R15). Transfer wire to the tub. Finish off with a small star on top.
5. If desired,when dry,decorate the tree with loops and bulbs of coloured Royal Icing (OO tube).
   * If spaghetti is used then the whole decoration is edible.
   Happy Christmas!

21

22

23

24

How to make the Fantasy Flower *(See Illustration 22)*

1. This can be made using any of the Calyx cutters (R11,R12,or R13)- R13 is shown. Make a small hook in the end of a piece of 28 gauge wire.

2. Using the 'Mexican Hat' method cut out one set of petals from flowerpaste with Minor Calyx Cutter R13 (See Illustration 23).
Place petal side on your hand and soften the edges with the balling tool (OP 1).Ball each petal towards the centre. Apply 'glue' (egg white,gum arabic or rose water) to the hook on the wire and push the wire gently through the centre of the flower. Make a hollow in the centre of the flower with the balling tool.
Slim the stem by rolling between your index fingers. Cut off excess paste.

3. Roll out more flowerpaste and cut out one flat set of petals with the R13 cutter(See Illustration 24). Soften the edges and ball towards the centre to cup them. Apply glue to the hollow in the centre of the flower and push the centre of the newly cupped petals into the hollow. Make sure the petals interleave.

4. Pop some stamens into the centre with tweezers. 'Sparkle' stamens add a touch of glamour!
Dust the edges of the petals and base of the stem with petal dust. Decorate as required. Bend the wire over if required.

26

27

How to make the Freesia Flower (See Illustration 25)

1. Select one long stamen which is just shorter than the length of one petal,cut off the head,soften the end in water,flatten it and fan out. Cut the end into 4/5 sections with sharp scissors and tape onto a piece of 26 gauge wire together with 3 shorter stamens. Put a small piece of paste around the base of the stamens.

2. Roll out the paste and, using the Freesia cutter (F1), cut out a flat set of petals and soften the edges on both sides with the balling tool(OP 1).
Flute slightly - that is lay the petal over your finger and ball lightly.
Press onto a dried maize leaf(corn on the cob) to vein it. (See Page 31).
Dust the centre and slightly up the petals with petal dust using a soft brush - colouring of choice.

3. Place onto a piece of soft sponge dusted with cornflour and,laying a knitting needle along the length of each petal,roll lightly from side to side to round the petal.
Apply a little 'glue' (egg white,gum arabic or rose water) to the piece of paste at the base of the stamens on the wire and push the wire through the centre of the petals just made. Hang upside down (See Illustration 26).

4. Make a 'Mexican Hat' of paste with a thin throat (See Illustration 27) and cut a second set of petals complete with throat. Shape petals as before and then push a cocktail stick down the throat and press against your thumb to thin out the paste

5. Apply glue to the base of the first set of petals on the wire and push the wire down the throat of the second set so that the two sets of petals nestle together,making sure that the second set of petals lie between the first set,giving a flower with six petals.
Roll the stem between your fingers to thin out the paste and remove any excess,then re-smooth.
Hang upside down to dry.

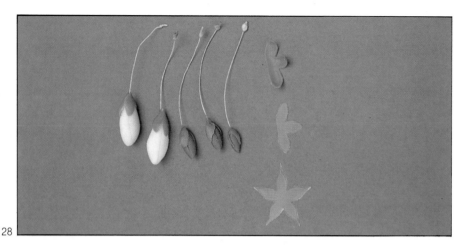

28

How to make a Freesia Bud *(See Illustration 28).*

6. Wrap a small tapered sausage of coloured flower paste round a glued stamen,green if tiny,flower coloured if larger, and mark the sides with a knife.
7. Roll out some green paste and cut out a Minor Calyx(R13). Cut off two of the sepals and the tips of the remaining sepals. Soften edges with the balling tool (OP1) and ball towards the centre to cup it.
   Apply a spot of glue to the calyx and wrap round bud.
   Tape to main stem as required.

29

How to make the Blossoms *(See Illustration 29)*

1. Roll out coloured flowerpaste thinly and press firmly down with the Blossom cutter (F2). Turn the complete piece of paste over onto a cornfloured sponge and push out each blossom in turn by pressing gently in the centre of each with the balling tool (OP 1).(See Illustration 30). This will automatically cup them. Turning the paste over gives a finer edge to the finished blossom. Try it out for yourself to see the difference!

2. Push a hat pin through the centre of each blossom in turn,leaving them on the hat pin,and tapping gently to separate them. Leave to dry. If you take them off too soon they will lose their shape.
   Repeat the above proceedure until you have the required number.

3. When dry, cut some stamens in half and thread through the centre of each blossom. Put a little 'glue'(egg white,gum arabic or rose water) under the head of the stamen and make certain that the stamen is stuck to the blossom. Leave to dry.

4. To assemble. Cut florists tape into 3 lengthwise. Cut the top of one piece at an angle and wrap the end round the top of a piece of 28-32 gauge wire. Tuck a blossom stamen between the wire and the extended tape.Hold the wire between the index finger and thumb of your left hand and roll the wire with your thumb along your index finger,at the same time holding the tape taut at an angle of 45°. Gradually add more blossoms as you go down the wire.
   These should be wired in multiples of 3,5 & 7 or grouped in bunches.
   3 taped stamens on their own act as buds.

How to make the Blossom Pattern *(See Illustration 31)*

1. This is just one way of making use of this very quick method of decoration. While the plaque or cake surface is still soft press the Blossom cutter (F2) gently into the required positions leaving the outline of 5 blossoms. Press a pointed fluted tool(or a 42/43 Beckenal star tube) into the centre of each blossom and then dust the indentations with petal dust using a soft brush.

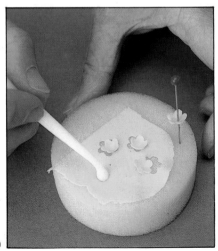

30

31

32

33

How to make the Primrose *(See Illustration 32)*

1. Tape one pale yellow stamen to the end of a piece of 26 gauge wire and,using egg white,gum arabic or rose water as glue,attach a small piece of yellow flower paste to the bottom of the stamen.
2. Make a 'Mexican Hat' of yellow flower paste and, using the Small Primrose cutter (F3), cut out a flower complete with throat.(See Illustration 33).
   Push a cocktail stick well down into the throat and roll between your index fingers to thin down the throat. Open out the centre more by rotating the cocktail stick. Apply a little glue to the paste on the wire and push the wire into the throat until the end of the stamen is just below the opening in the centre. Glue a small piece of green paste to the base of the throat.
3. Roll out green paste thinly and cut out a Minor Calyx (R13).
   Cut off 2 sepals, cut down the centre of two adjacent sepals and spread out. Ball towards the centre with the balling tool (OP1) to cup, and vein with a maize leaf. Apply a little glue to the base of the stem and wrap the calyx round.
   Dust the centre of the flower with Egg Yellow petal dust on a soft brush.

How to make the Primrose Leaves *(See Illustration 32)*

1. Using a reverse Primrose Leaf mould,made as directed on Page 30, make the leaf as directed on Page 31. Dry over the end of a wooden spoon to obtain the curved effect. Bend to the required shape before completely dry.

34

How to make the Miniature Rose *(See Illustration 34)*

(Patience is required!)

1. 'Glue' a small cone of flowerpaste to the hooked end of a piece of 28/30 gauge wire. Use egg white,gum arabic or rose water as the glue.Leave to set.
2. Roll out white flowerpaste and cut out 3 flowers,one thicker than the other two, using the Small Primrose cutter (F3). Colour with petal dust using a soft brush,yellow in the centre and rose colour on the outside.
3. Place the first flower on your hand,soften the edges and ball all 5 petals with the balling tool(OP 1) to cup them. Make cuts along the side of each petal about ½ way in from the tips of the petals to the centre. This is to make them more flexible for the next stage.(See Illustration 35).
4. Thread the wire through the centre,apply glue to the flowerpaste cone and press up the two opposite petals (No's 1 & 3) (See Illustration 36) tightly round the cone.(See Illustration 37).
   Bend up the remaining three petals,apply glue to the edges and interlock them round the centre. Tweezers can be used if necessary. Hang upsidedown on rack.

35

36

5. Turn over the second flower and lightly ball each petal just inside the edge to cup them. Turn back and ball the centre of each petal taking care not to lose the shape of the cupped edge.
Glue the base of the first flower and slide the second onto the wire until it nestles round the first. Apply glue to the edges and interlock the second row of petals with each other.

6. Ball the petals of the third flower(the thickest) front and back exactly like the second flower. Glue the base of second row and slide the third flower onto the wire until it nestles round the second. Interlock the third row of petals with each other.
Dust and darken the centre of the rose.
Glue a small piece of green paste onto the base of the flower to form the rose hip.

7. Roll out green & white flowerpaste,one on top of the other, and cut out a small calyx using the R15 cutter.
Cut spikes on each sepal (See Illustration 38). Ball lightly,glue the base of the rose and slide the calyx up the wire,white side up, until it folds round the base of the rose.

8. Mark round the base of the flower with a knife to emphasise the rose hip and arrange the sepals artistically. If using coloured paste for the flower,make each row of petals a different shade,using the darker shade in the centre and the lightest shade on the outside.

How to make small Rose Leaves (See Illustration 38).

9. Roll out green flowerpaste and cut out the smallest rose leaf using the R7 cutter. This is too big for the miniature rose so cut it down to size by, still using the R7 cutter,moving the cutter down a little and cutting off the top of the leaf. Then move it sideways slightly and cut off the side of the leaf. Repeat for the opposite side.

10. Vein the leaf by using a portion of the R10 leaf mould.

Our more recent Mini Rose Leaf (R17) can also be used.

39

How to make the Miniature Wired Briar Rose *(See Illustration 39)*

1. The Calyx. Roll out some green flowerpaste and cut out a small calyx(R15). Cut spikes on each sepal as for the miniature rose (See Illustration 40). Cup by balling with the balling tool(OP 1) on your dusted hand from the tips of the sepals towards the centre,taking care not to break the spikes. Cup in the centre by gently pressing into a soft cornfloured sponge. Make a small hole in the centre to take a wire and leave to set in the bowl of a small measuring spoon.

2. The Flower. Roll out some white flowerpaste thinly and cut out a flower using the Small Primrose cutter (F3). Lightly dust the centre with Apple Green and the outside edge with Mod Red petal dust using a soft brush. Gently smooth the edges with the balling tool.

40

3. Turn the flower over and ball just under the edge of each petal,which will make it cup. Turn over again,place the whole flower onto soft cornfloured sponge and curve all the petals up by pressing gently with the balling tool from centre of petal to centre of flower,taking care not to lose the shape on the cupped edge.
4. Lightly glue the centre of the calyx (use egg white,gum arabic or rose water) and place the flower into it,making sure that each petal centre is over the edge of a sepal.
5. Make a small hook in the end of a piece of 28/30 gauge wire and bend the hook over to one side. Apply glue to the hook and thread the rose onto the wire,making sure it is firmly pressed into the centre of the flower. Hang upsidedown to dry completely.
6. Stamens. Cut approx.12/15 stamens to unequal lengths. Add a little egg white/rose water to some pale yellow flowerpaste(to make it a little softer and stickier). Take a tiny ball of this paste,flatten slightly,dampen centre of rose with glue and press in the ball. Insert the longer stamens,with tweezers, into the ball N,S,E & W with the shorter ones in between making sure the effect is kept uneven. Keep the centre clear.
7. Stick a very small ball of pale green paste right in the centre to complete the rose.

How to make Buds for the Briar Rose *(See Illustration 39)*
1. Glue a minute ball of flowerpaste to the hooked end of a piece of 28/30 gauge wire(use egg white,gum arabic or rose water). Leave to dry completely.
2. Roll out white flowerpaste and cut out one flower using the Small Primrose cutter(F3). Lightly dust the edges with Mod Red petal dust using a soft brush.
3. Ball all 5 petals on your dusted hand. Make cuts along the side of each petal about 1/2 way in from the tips of the petals to the centre. This is to make them more flexible for the next stage.
4. Thread the wire through the centre and apply glue to the flowerpaste ball. Press up 2 opposite petals (No's 2 & 5) tightly round the ball.Bend up the remaining 3 petals,one at a time,apply glue to one edge of each and interlock them round the centre. Tweezers might be useful. Hang upsidedown on a rack and dry thoroughly.
5. Glue a small piece of green paste onto the base of the bud to form the rose hip.
6. Roll out some green flowerpaste and cut out a small calyx using the R15 cutter. Cut spikes on each sepal(See Illustration 40) and ball lightly. Glue the base and sides of the bud and slide the calyx up the wire and fold it around the bud.
7. Mark round the rose hip with a knife where it joins the bud,to emphasise the shape of the rose hip. Allow to dry completely.

41

42

43

How to make the Miniature Carnation *(See Illustration 41)*

1. Roll out pale pink flowerpaste thinly and cut out 2 or 3 shapes with the Small Primrose cutter (F3). The number depends on the fullness of the carnation you wish to make.
   Cut one large nick in the centre of each heart with a sharp knife, and 2 or 3 shorter cuts each side. Flute the edges of all petals with a cocktail stick(See Illustration 42).

2. Make a small hook on the end of a piece of 28/30 gauge wire. Put a little glue(egg white,gum arabic or rose water) on the hook and thread the wire through the centre of a petal. Pressing at the base ,fold the petal in half. Put a little more glue onto the petal and fold $\frac{1}{3}$ to the front and $\frac{1}{3}$ to the back, squeezing at the base. (See Illustration 43).

3. Apply glue to the base of the petal and slightly higher in a few places.Insert the wire through the centre of the second petal and squeeze the second petal round the centre of the first. Make sure you do not touch the tops of the petals or you will not obtain that 'natural' look.

4. Repeat the process of the second petal for the third if a fuller carnation is required.
   When dry brush the tips of the petals with a darker shade of pink petal dust.

44

How to make the Miniature Daisy *(See Illustration 44)*

1. Calyx. Glue a small ball of green paste onto the hooked end of a piece of 28/30 gauge wire using egg white,gum arabic or rose water. Roll gently between your fingers to form a tiny sausage. Holding the sausage between your fingers,near the hook,press gently on the top with the balling tool to form a tiny cup. Allow to dry.

2. Flower. Roll out white flowerpaste thinly and cut out a flower using the Small Primrose cutter (F3). Cut each petal in two lengthways with a sharp knife as far as the base of the cut edge,but no further.
Cut at each join between petals ½ way to the centre of the flower,but no further.
Put the flower on your hand and dust the tips with petal dust as required.
Lay a cocktail stick along each petal in turn and rock from side to side to curl the petals slightly. Flick alternate petals up slightly.

3. Place on a sponge and indent the centre with the balling tool. Apply glue to the calyx cup and ,holding the flower on your finger upsidedown,attach the wired calyx. Press in the centre with the balling tool to make sure the flower is attached to the calyx. Adjust petals to look as realistic as possible.Hang up to dry completely.

4. Centre. Cut a small ball of yellow paste in half and stick onto the end of a cocktail stick. Apply glue and dip into yellow mealie meal, semolina, gelatine,coloured caster sugar or mark with tulle to represent pollen(See Illustration 45). Dampen the centre of the daisy with glue and attach the centre. Adjust petals again.

45

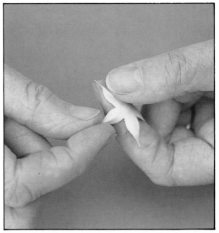

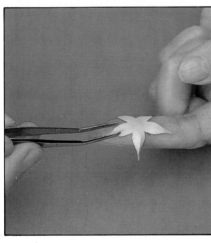

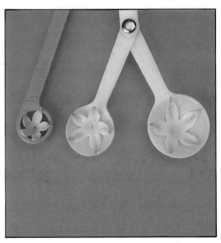

46

47

48

49

How to make the Blushing Bride *(See Illustration 46)*

1. Use very pale,almost white,pink flowerpaste. Glue a tiny ball of paste onto the hooked end of a piece of 26/28 gauge wire with egg white,gum arabic or rose water. Leave to dry.

2. Roll out some paste thinly and cut out 3 flowers using the Calyx cutters R11,R12 & R13. Soften the edges of the petals and thin with the balling tool (OP 1). Form a crease down the back of each petal(squeeze with your fingers to get a firm crease)(See Illustration 47) or use tweezers (gently)(See Illustration 48). Turn over and lightly ball each petal from point to centre to cup flower.

   Lay the flower on a sponge and make a small hole in the centre for the wire. Dry thoroughly in a curved position such as in a measuring spoon(See Illustration 49). Using petal dust and a soft brush blush the back of each petal,the vein on the front and the tip of each petal with pink. The centre of the flower is a soft green. Do not be lavish with the colour.

50

51

3. Centre. For the centre cut out 2 more R13 calyxes and soften the edges, both sides, with the large end of the balling tool. Gently rub the edges thinner with the small end. Cut the end of each petal as many times as possible with a sharp knife starting in the centre and working outwards.(See Illustration 50). Stroke the edges of the petals with a Mod Red colour until the tips are pink in colour.

4. Apply glue to the centre ball and slide the first centre flower up the wire and squeeze round so that the ball does not show(See Illustration 51). Blush the outside edges of the petals. Apply glue to the base of the flower and slide the second flower up the wire and attach by gently squeezing the base. Blush the outside of the top of the petals gently. Blush the base with Apple Green.

5. Taking the dry No.13 flower blush the front & back of the centre with green. Gently blush the centre veins and grooves up to the top with Mod Red using a 000 brush to give a delicate pink effect.
Glue a minute piece of pale green paste to the base of the flower,apply glue to that and slide the size 13 flower up the wire and attach.
Colour the size 12 flower in the same way, glue a small piece of paste to the base of the flower and attach the size 12 flower with the petals lying in between those of the size 13 flower.

6. Repeat the process for the final size 11 flower.
In its natural state this flower darkens with age but looks loveliest in the gentle colours.

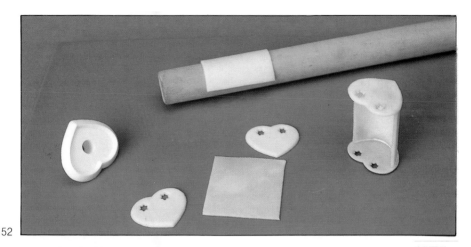

52

53

How to make the Heart-shaped Crib *(See Illustration 52)*

1. Roll out some white flowerpaste and cut out 2 heart shapes using the Briar Rose cutter (R14). Cut out a square 1½'' x 1½'' * and set over a ¾'' dia. pin or dowel. Leave to dry.
2. Lay one heart shape on a board and attach one end of the curved portion of the base piece to it with thick Royal Icing. Royal Ice the other end of the curved portion and attach the other heart shape to it, lining it up carefully. Decorate as required. Attach to plaque or cake with Royal Icing.
3. * Templates. If you prefer to work from templates for this sort of thing, then cut them out with scissors from a plastic icecream container for longer life. This also ensures that the material will meet with the EEC Food Regulations. In addition,to keep sharp knives away from the template,try laying the template onto the soft paste and rolling over it with your rolling pin. You can then cut round the resulting indentation very easily.(See Illustration 53).

54

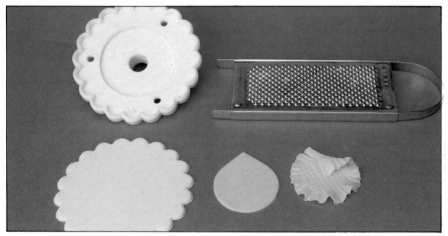

55

4. To fill the Crib (See Illustration 54)
   To make the mattress,take a sausage of paste and flatten it in the crib.
   Take a small ball of white paste,flatten slightly and form into a pillow.Indent for the baby's head.
5. Roll out some white paste and cut out a petal shape,to make the cot cover,using the Rose Petal cutter R1. Using the nutmeg grater,indent a pattern onto the lower 2/3rds of the cover. Turn the cover over and indent a pattern on the upper 1/3rd. Flute the edge with a cocktail stick. Turn the cover over again and flute the edge of the lower 2/3rds.Fold down the upper portion.(See Illustration 55).
6. Make a complete moulded baby or mould just its head and use a sausage of paste under the cover to represent its body.Tuck the cover round baby while still soft. Dust with petal dust to suit.
7. The complete cradle can be attached with Royal Icing to a plaque cut with a Garrett Frill cutter.

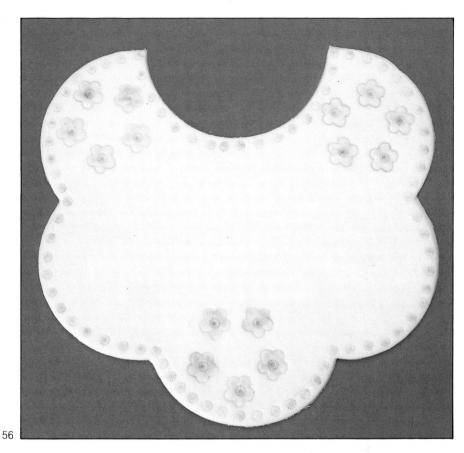

56

How to make the Baby's Bib *(See Illustration 56)*

Roll out Sugarpaste,Flowerpaste or Pastillage using spacers,if you like,under each end of the rolling pin to give an even thickness and cut out a plaque using the base of the Rose Set petal shaped box. Cut out the neck with a $2^3/8''$ dia. cutter. Make an indentation in three of the petal shapes with the Blossom cutter (F2). Make indentations around the edges and in the centres of the blossoms with a Beckenal No.43 piping tube.
When dry petal dust the indentations.

57

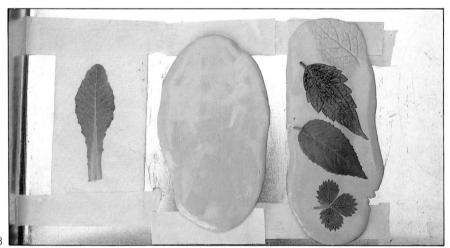

58

How to make Leaf Veiners *(See Illustration 57)*

1. You will need;- Well veined fresh leaves (make sure they are clean & dry).
   'Milliput' epoxy putty - standard grade * (See Page 30)
   Vaseline
   2″wide Masking Tape
   Shallow tray
2. Method. Cut masking tape slightly longer than the leaf. Place in the tray with the sticky side UP and hold flat with two smaller pieces top and bottom. Lightly vaseline the tray round the edges of the masking tape to prevent sticking. Place the face of the leaf onto the sticky tape and smooth out from the centre with your fingers to remove any air bubbles or creases. Leave a small piece of stalk for easier handling (See Illustration 58).

59

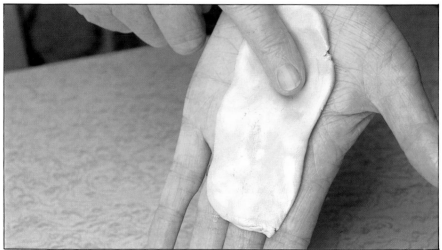

60

3. Cut equal lengths (about 2″) from each of the Milliput packs. Rub a small amount of vaseline onto your hands and knead the two pieces of Milliput together until they are a uniform colour(See Illustration 59).
Press out some of the Milliput into a flat sheet,slightly larger than the leaf and about 3mm (¹/₈″) thick.
Smear a little vaseline over one face of the Milliput and place that side on top of the leaf. Press firmly onto the leaf. Put a little vaseline on your fingers and smooth the upper surface (See Illustration 60).
4. For economy you can now use the upper surface to make another veiner by placing a second leaf with its underside onto the Milliput. Smooth out from the centre as before. Leave to set overnight. Additional heat is not required.

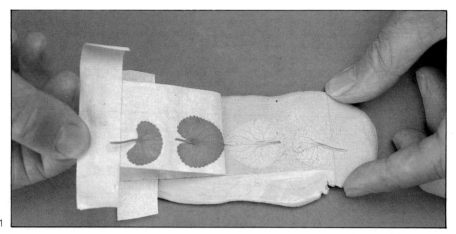

61

62

5. When set peel off the upper leaf, and then peel off the masking tape underneath which will remove the lower leaf as well. (See Illustration 61)

6. Reverse Veiner. The underside or back of the leaf is used to make the veiner because it gives much clearer veining. This gives an embossed effect on the sugar paste, which is not often required. Therefore it is usually necessary to make a 'reverse veiner' in the same manner. (See Illustration 62)

Lightly vaseline a flat piece of Milliput and press onto the veiner you have just made and allowed to set, pressing in firmly. Peel off straight away.

Check that the veiner is satisfactory and leave to set overnight on a vaselined tray.

Happy veiner making!

7. *Milliput is non-toxic once it has set. It sets rock hard by chemical action once mixed but remains workable for about an hour. Therefore you should mix only smallish quantities at one time. It is available from good toy or model shops or direct from ORCHARD PRODUCTS.

63

How to use the Veiners *(See Illustration 63)*

8. Lightly dust the veiner with cornflour. (If using a fat based paste then this step will not be necessary.)
9. Roll out some green flowerpaste slightly larger than the leaf and press into the veiner with the heel of your hand. Peel off and cut round the edge of the leaf shape with a knife. Smooth the edges with the balling tool (OP 1). Curl to the required shape and leave to dry.

64

How to prepare a Maize (Corn on the Cob) Leaf as a veiner. *(See Illustration 64).*

1. Dry thoroughly - until it goes white - about a week. Reinforce the back by sticking masking tape all over to preserve the shape. The tapered end gives a different style of veining to the flatter part.

ANOTHER RECIPE

Flowerpaste C.
450g icing sugar
15ml Gum Tragacanth
10ml gelatine soaked in 25ml of cold water
45ml egg white
20g white vegetable fat

Grease the inside of a large mixing bowl with fat and place on top of a pot of hot water. The bottom of the bowl should not touch the water.
Sift half the icing sugar with the Gum Trag. into the mixing bowl.
Place the pot on the heat and bring the water to the boil to warm the mixture.
Put the soaked gelatine in a small container over hot water to dissolve and clarify, DO NOT boil.
Remove the mixing bowl from the heat and pour the egg white and dissolved gelatine into a well you make in the icing sugar. Stir into the mixture gradually. Beat very well until white and creamy.
Pour the rest of the icing sugar into a 2nd bowl and warm through in an oven. Alternatively, using a non-metallic bowl, warm it in a microwave oven. Give it 3 periods of 50 seconds on full, stirring in between. Do not heat continuously as a crust will form. Add the warm icing sugar to the mixture gradually to make a smooth paste.
Knead the paste on your non-stick board adding small pieces of the remainder of the fat gradually until smooth, elastic and cold.
Put in a plastic bag in an airtight container and leave to rest for 24 hours.
Work through every 2/3 days.

STOP PRESS!
1. A unique 3-in-1 Garrett Frill Cutter with 3 interchangeable plug-in centre cutters.
2. A unique Carnation Cutter which cuts out the little indentations for you, AND gives you a fluted centre cutter for the Garrett Frill!
3. A set of 4 Holly leaves which have been copied from nature as closely as possible and do not follow the usual artistic impression.
4. A set of 4 delightful Ivy Leaves, again taken from nature.
Read about them in Book 3!
5. There are now six books in this series Nos. 1 to 6.
Many other cutters have been added to the range. Read all about them in Books 3, 4, 5 and 6.